CW00435179

FOR JERUSALEM'S SAKE I WILL NOT REST

By the same author:

A FORETASTE OF HEAVEN (Autobiography)
ALLAH OR THE GOD OF THE BIBLE –
   WHAT IS THE TRUTH?
BEHOLD HIS LOVE
FATHER OF COMFORT (Daily Readings)
HIDDEN IN HIS HANDS
IF I ONLY LOVE JESUS
IN OUR MIDST – JESUS LOVES AND SUFFERS TODAY
IN WHOM THE FATHER DELIGHTS
ISRAEL MY CHOSEN PEOPLE
MARY, THE MOTHER OF JESUS
MORE PRECIOUS THAN GOLD (Daily Readings)
MY ALL FOR HIM
PATMOS – WHEN THE HEAVENS OPENED
PRAYING OUR WAY THROUGH LIFE
REALITIES – THE MIRACLES OF GOD EXPERIENCED TODAY
REPENTANCE – THE JOY-FILLED LIFE
RULED BY THE SPIRIT
THE BLESSINGS OF ILLNESS
THE CHRISTIAN'S VICTORY
THE EVE OF PERSECUTION
THE HIDDEN TREASURE IN SUFFERING
THE UNSEEN WORLD OF ANGELS AND DEMONS
WHAT COMES AFTER DEATH? –
   THE REALITY OF HEAVEN AND HELL

FOR JERUSALEM'S SAKE
I WILL NOT REST

BASILEA SCHLINK

Marshall Pickering

Marshall Morgan and Scott
Marshall Pickering
3 Beggarwood Lane, Basingstoke, Hants. RG23 7LP

Copyright © Evangelical Sisterhood of Mary, 1969

Original title: UM JERUSALEMS WILLEN
First German edition 1968
First English edition 1969
Reprinted 1971
Reprinted 1973
Reprinted 1976
Re-issued 1986

Cover photo:
View of the Golden Gate, Jerusalem, from the Garden
of Gethsemane.

ISBN 0 551 00741 9

Printed and bound in Great Britain by
Anchor Brendon Limited, Tiptree, Essex

CONTENTS

FOREWORD:
THE PATH OF ISRAEL — A VISION

The impetus for this book is an inner vision, which God gave for Israel, His beloved people. Because we love God, we love His people also.* In 1940 the Lord showed Mother Basilea from His Word what the path of His people Israel was to be. Although Hitler had already formed his plan for the extermination of Israel, God made it clear to Mother Basilea that Israel had a future. He showed her that His people would not perish, but rather would be saved and would return home to the land of their fathers. It was the era of National Socialism; one was not permitted to mention the name "Israel" in a positive sense. Still, Mother Basilea was driven by the burden which God had laid upon her heart. She spent seven years lecturing in German cities, both large and small, bearing witness to the fact that Israel would still be the people of blessing for all

---

* Let the reader remember that it is not the author's intention to describe God's plan for the last days in detail, but rather only to draw upon those aspects which directly pertain to Israel.

peoples. Some people probably thought that what she was saying was sheer madness. It certainly was madness to say such things in public, when one considered that it was possible to be imprisoned in a concentration camp or sentenced to death. But Mother Basilea knew that she was in the Lord's hands, which are stronger than all political powers and which would protect her, if He wanted to preserve her for another task.

Even though Mother Basilea was twice summoned before the Gestapo because of this biblical proclamation, she experienced the Lord's protection. God confirmed the message which He had given her: Israel did not perish as other peoples have perished and as it was planned for this people. Israel could not be exterminated; rather she rose up again as a people and became a nation, which almost all nations have recognized.

After the founding of the Sisterhood of Mary in 1947, God molded the inner life of the sisterhood in such a manner, that we came to love His people with a deeper and greater love through repentance of the crime which our German people had committed against Israel. He gave Mother Basilea the commission to call our people to the repentance of this sin. Out of this concern in 1958 she wrote the book,

"Israel — My Chosen People," which was translated into three other languages in the same year. Because of its timely content, thousands of copies were sold. In this book Mother Basilea could not help but show again how powerful the call of Israel as God's chosen people is and how very much this has become apparent in our times. She described how through Israel all the nations of the earth would be blessed in the last days. In a similar manner she embodied both the call to repentance for the Germans and God's plan of salvation for Israel in the herald play "Israel," which we have presented to thousands in most of the large cities of the Federal Republic of Germany and also in neighboring countries.

In later writings Mother Basilea elaborated on the end-time theme, pointing out the significance of developments in the world scene. Explaining according to the Holy Scriptures how the most important international events would take place in Jerusalem, she bore witness again that Israel would not be destroyed, but that God would prepare her for His commission in the Messianic Kingdom of the last days.

That this is coming to pass we saw clearly during the Six Day War in June, 1967. When the war broke out, it became evident to Mother Basilea from all the prophecies for the last days in which we are living: Israel will win! Therefore, two days before the beginning of the war she wrote to our friends in Israel: "Israel will not die, but will live ... God is with His people and will save them ... Israel will experience miracles ..."[1] And Israel did experience miracles and did have victory, because God promised it and because He fought for Israel.

When Mother Basilea wrote these words with the Israelis and our Jewish brothers outside of Israel in mind, she knew that it would be presumptuous to do so as a non-Jew and especially as a German, if the clear call of God had not been there. Still, as God had commanded her to proclaim the message, which He had given her during the era of National Socialism in defiance of the government, so now she is compelled to be obedient to God and to proclaim this message to His beloved, chosen people. Through obedience to God and love to the people of Israel she must complete this task.

During the time of the greatest threat to Israel, June 1967, we — Mother Basilea and I and all of our spiritual daughters — sensed how great our love for Israel is. Israel's anguish became our anguish; we became united with her, as if she were our own flesh and blood. Our hearts trembled for the sake of Israel, for the sake of our many friends there, and, of course, for the sake of our sisters in Talpiot, whose house lay close to the border and therefore also in the line of fire. (Later we heard that troops were fighting only a few hundred yards from their house during the critical hours.)

During the time of this great threat to Israel, God laid such a heavy burden upon our hearts that we prayed and pleaded for Israel to an extent that we had never dreamt possible. God gave us more than natural strength, so that all the sisters were able to come together to pray to the living God at 5 a. m. before the beginning of the day's work. Real battles of prayer were fought for His people. Yes, it was like Jacob's wrestling with the angel, as we continued to fight in prayer for weeks afterward at every further threat to Israel. We could sense how the world of angels fought with us, how the heavens were stirred. In the afternoons and evenings we continued to fight battles of prayer. We also sang songs of victory for the victories which the Lord had already given and which He would continue to give. Because Israel's anguish had become our anguish, Israel's joy also became our joy and we raised our voices together in songs of praise for what the Lord had done for His people.

Because our hearts throb for Israel, Mother Basilea cannot help but proclaim the message which God gave her in a vision of the future. We are deeply convinced that the future of Israel — her preservation or her suffering — depends upon her relationship to God during the coming times. Mother Basilea is trying to lead Israel to the proper inner attitude through this book.

May we sense Mother Basilea's love of Israel, of the people and of the country, in everything that she writes. Here she is concerned with what God has spoken to His people through His prophets about the future path of Israel, what He has called Israel to be and how He offers her aid and deliverance. Attention is first centered on the general situation of the world, so that Israel's special position might be brought into sharper focus.

The Word of God and an inner compulsion have driven Mother Basilea as a Christian to write this book with our Israeli friends in mind. We pray that it may serve its purpose — namely to work for the salvation of Israel.

Mother Martyria   November 1967

ISRAEL AT THE TURNING-POINT OF THE LAST DAYS

Innumerable signs announce the hour in which
we are living. After 2000 years the incomprehensible has happened: the Jews have
returned home and are living again in the land
of their fathers, which God granted to them
as their eternal possession, when He solemnly
promised it to Abraham.[2] According to prophetic declarations — in Ezekiel,[3] for example
— their return home would take place in the
"last days." That is why their home-coming
is a sign of the last days. That Jerusalem is in
the hands of the Jews is also a sign that prophecy will be fulfilled, for it is written that
Jerusalem will be besieged, because God's
people live there.[4]

Because God has shown His miraculous power
in Israel — as He did during the events of the
Six Day War — Israel has been placed in the
limelight as the people by whom God stands,
as the people who are God's chosen people.
That is also a sign of the last days, prophesied
by Ezekiel: "My holy name I will make known
in the midst of my people Israel; and I will not

let my holy name be profaned any more; and the nations shall know that I am the Lord, the Holy One in Israel."[5]

The Arabian countries and the communist countries, especially the Soviet Union and China, are seeking to annihilate Israel. They are the godless nations, which fight for their atheistic ideology and which have already brought more than one-third of the world's population under their influence — yes, some even speak of two-thirds. The fight of the godless Goliath against the small God-fearing David is one of the main themes which will come to a climax in this drama. Again, this is a fulfillment of the prophetic declarations for the last days.[6]

Our times have another characteristic of the end of time: threats and rumors of war beset the world. Peace has disappeared from the earth; nations hate each other and fight each other as never before. There is a possibility of a third world war — with atomic weapons. We are living in a time like none before. The well-known nuclear physicist Philberth writes:*
"In the whole history of the earth and of mankind there was never such a time, as the one which has manifested itself over the past

* Bernhard Philberth, "Christian Prophecy and Nuclear Energy," Glock and Lutz, Nuremberg, 1961.

few decades ... Never before were the pre-
requisites there so that catastrophes, which
can encompass and destroy the whole globe,
could be brought about by the hand of man,
i. e. by atomic weapons ... Up until now
every catastrophe was limited in area ...
Never before were the peace and safety of the
whole world so problematic and uncertain and
threatened by such a sudden and violent end
as today." Destruction threatens to explode
over the whole earth with dreadful devastation, such as the world has never seen before.
People all over the earth will become more and
more consumed by dread as they fearfully
await the things, which will come over all the
inhabitants of the earth and from which there
is no escape. For mankind has become one
large family — a war, which breaks out in one
place, concerns all nations since it can develop
into a world-wide fire.

Today the words of the prophet Jeremiah are
being fulfilled: "Behold evil is going forth
from nation to nation, and a great tempest is
stirring from the farthest parts of the earth!"[7]
— a further sign of the last days. The period
of grace is reaching an end; the wrath of God
is about to explode over the world; catastrophe will follow upon catastrophe: wars, earth-
quakes, devastations. This outburst of divine

wrath concerns, above all, mankind, which is approaching judgment.

The prophecy of Isaiah describes this age: "The earth is violently shaken. The earth staggers like a drunken man, it sways like a hut; its transgression lies heavy upon it, and it falls, and will not rise again."[8] What is the cause of such an unnerving event? The answer of the prophet is unequivocal: "Its transgression lies heavy upon it." — "The earth lies polluted under its inhabitants; for they have transgressed the laws, violated the statutes, broken the everlasting covenant. Therefore a curse devours the earth, and its inhabitants suffer for their guilt."[9]

Transgressions lay heavy upon the earth. The facts tell the story: the increasing number of crimes, of murders, of deeds of violence, of suicides, even of juvenile crimes, a phenomenon which had never before existed, — savage and uncontrollable passions, above all drug addiction and mass movements like the hippies — they describe the condition of the world today. These are the themes, which constantly occur in films, television programs and magazines, because this is what mankind wants to see and hear.

If mankind today finds its fulfillment in the satisfaction of all its carnal desires, then it will no longer have any inhibitions and will give full sway to its passions — hate, the urge to destroy, arrogance — to eradicate cities and entire nations with atomic weapons of destruction.

They themselves are guilty of the devastation which will break out over the earth. The urge to destroy has gripped men who have hidden their faces from God. Even in nursery schools, children, influenced by what they watch on television, make games out of killing, shooting and destroying. Men in their urge to destroy will be used as an instrument of the wrath of God, but insofar as the destruction which they cause falls back on themselves, they are also the object of the wrath of the Almighty.

When the earth can no longer bear her misdeeds, when apostasy and decadence have reached their peak, it will be as the prophet Isaiah prophesied: "Behold the day of the Lord comes, cruel with wrath and fierce anger, to make the earth a desolation and to destroy its sinners from it."[10] (Consider the effects of nuclear fall-out for wide areas of land from nuclear tests alone.) Moral decay has often been responsible for the fall of civilization. Decay always bears God's judgment. Both people and natural phenomena (hail and fire, for instance) will be instruments of God's judgment. The prophet Joel tells us that the stars will lose their lustre and the sun and moon will be darkened.[11] Let us not forget that God destroyed the world with a flood in the time of Noah. "Now the earth was corrupt in God's sight, and the earth was filled with violence."[12] Through corruption, mankind brought about its own annihilation.

Today it is again the case that the nations have drunk freely from the intoxicating cup of lewdness and passion.[13] They will rock to and fro under the influence of their lusts and sinful desires, like the inhabitants of Sodom and Gomorrah. In the last days this will bring about the day of the Lord, the day of His great wrath, which will descend like an avalanche on all those who are clinging to their earthly and evil desires — and perhaps very soon. Yes, today the prophetic word of Isaiah will be fulfilled: "For in a very little while my indignation will come to an end, and my anger will be directed to their destruction."[14]

THE GREAT TURNING-POINT

In this last hour, God's swift sword of judgment is ready to strike the world because of her crimes. The word of Zephaniah will be fulfilled: "On the day of the wrath of the Lord, in the fire of his jealous wrath, all the earth shall be consumed."[15] The apparent success of science and technology and of politics, yes even of humanitarian efforts, which may still come, cannot deceive us. We are standing at the turn of the tide, at the turning-point for the nations of the world, where the road of the display of power will end in destruction.

To be sure, in the course of history many world empires have perished, but never before have political catastrophes accumulated in such a manner nor have they had such a global effect as in the last few decades. The brilliance and wealth of the British Empire has disappeared. The United States of America is being pulverized by racial strife and the war in Vietnam, and finally by the conflict with enemies lurking behind the scenes.* On the

* Referring to the situation in 1967, when the book was written.

one hand stands China with her 700 million inhabitants and, on the other, the Soviet Union with her 230 million inhabitants. Their relationship with each other is tense and vehement. These eastern countries are coming to a period, where they will expend all of their resources on the war effort. That expenditure can quickly bring them to the end of their power, as the prophets have said the fate of the northern and eastern lands would be. So the events of the world foreshadow the downfall of the nations.

What significance does the end-time era hold for Israel? In comparision to other nations, her destiny will be unique. Certainly, she will be drawn into international conflicts, since many of the world events will concern her directly. However, during the last days she will not come to an utter end as will other nations. The history of Israel will take a different course.

On the one hand, the last days are the time of judgment for the nations, the time of gradual decline; but, on the other hand, they usher in a new era, a turning-point for Israel. The glory of the nations will end. Their display of power will bring about their decline. However, Israel will no longer live in disgrace. God's wrath will come to an end. During the last days God's sun of grace will begin to rise over Israel. The return home into her land, the reconstruction of the country, the taking of the whole city of Jerusalem with the wailing wall and the temple square, the occupation of the old holy places, e. g. the grave of the patriarch Abraham and the grave of Rachel — all of this signifies the beginning of a period of grace for Israel.

Yes, while the nations are following the road to destruction, Israel is receiving a new surge of life. (This does not mean that it will no longer become entangled in wars and threats of war.) Israel has arisen as a people and a nation, as a miraculous sign before the eyes of the whole world. It is the land of the future and of hope. Israel stands before the nations as a sign of grace, blessed by God through many miraculous, completely inexplicable victories during the Six Day War. If the situation were seen through human eyes alone, it would seem as though Israel's enemies held all the trump cards in their hands. And still the incomprehensible happened. Israel emerged as victor — because God fought for Israel, because He performed miracles similar to the ones He performed in biblical times.

What does this turn of events signify? The crucial point is that God has led Israel into a new phase of her history; He has changed

His relationship to her; He now stands by her. For two thousand years it seemed as though God was fighting against Israel. He humiliated her and led her along the path of correction, full of sufferings. He did not reply to the supplications of millions of His people in the dreadful concentration camps with His succour and with His miracles. Yet now He let the same members of His people, who experienced those dreadful times, witness His aid and His answer to their prayers during the Six Day War. For the human mind it is an incomprehensible change in the history and life of Israel.

THE PLAN ENCOMPASSES
THOUSANDS OF YEARS

How are we to understand this turning-point?
Is God an inconsistent God? Is He an arbit-
rary God, Who humiliates His people and lets
them suffer dreadful things for two thousand
years and then suddenly showers them with
grace and prosperity? Or is there a special
plan hidden in these contradictory events, a
plan laid down in eternity?
Yes, an eternal plan of God lies behind these
seemingly contradictory events. This plan is
revealed to us. We can read it with our own
eyes. It was written down thousands of years
ago.
Up until now the entire history of Israel has
been carried out according to this plan. Piece
by piece the plan has been realized and it will
lead to a glorious and magnificent end. The
plan of God is unequivocally determined. The
eternal God has chosen and appointed Israel
to be a peerless people and has laid upon her
shoulders an immense commission for the
whole world. God has chosen this people to
bring prosperity and salvation to all peoples

and a light unto all nations.[16] All peoples will receive salvation through Israel. She will become the Messianic Kingdom, into which all the peoples of the world will be drawn and of whose blessing they should all partake.

Because God is not a despot, but rather a loving Father, Israel, His partner, must take part in the execution of this plan. He enters into a covenant of mutual love and dedication with His chosen people, to whom He has given such a great commission.

Even in a human marital covenant, it should be the case that the wife dedicates her whole life to her husband, that she is one with him in heart and soul, that she is bound to him in love, that she is at his disposal, caught up in his work and destiny. Just as the Lord has ordained this to be the proper relationship between man and wife, He has ordained this to be the proper relationship between Himself and His people. With the establishment of the covenant, Israel should take His commandments, the proclamations of His will, into their hearts with love. They should live, act and carry out their commission according to these proclamations.

The establishment of such a covenant of most intimate fellowship does not mean simply the fulfilling of external laws, but rather, a complete dedication of the heart. As Moses said, "Circumcise therefore the foreskin of your heart . . ."[17] What a wondrous, powerful hour, when God first made a covenant with the patriarch Abraham and disclosed His plan with the unimaginable promise: "By you all the families of the earth shall bless themselves."[18]

What a prodigious, great and eternally meaningful hour it was on Mount Sinai, as God solemnly established His covenant with His people. There He called them to be His holy people, the bearer of blessing for all the world through the proclamation of His Ten Commandments. Thomas Mann once said: "All the law books of the world are nothing but interpretations or commentaries of the Ten Commandments." What a prodigious hour, in which God again declared unto His servant Israel through His prophets: "I will give you as a light to the nations."[19] God gave everything to this people. They are the object of His love. He revealed Himself to them through the proclamation of His will in the Ten Commandments. He disclosed to them His very Being, so that they could proclaim to all the world, Who He is.

But then came the great disappointment for the Lord! His people did not live up to His expectations, to the hope, which He had placed in them. They did not reply to His love, wherein there is strength to accomplish great things for God and the world. They did not accept the offer of grace. They showed themselves unworthy of their great and incomprehensible election. For the people of Israel did not enter into the proclamations of the will of their Lord. They did not love Him with all their heart and with all their mind. Yes, they broke this covenant and made covenants with other gods — served evil and did evil, so that the land was filled with transgressions and crimes. Therefore, God lamented and spoke through His prophet Jeremiah: "Your wickedness will chasten you, and your apostasy will reprove you."[20] Israel was not only guilty for her sin of commission, but also for her sin of omission. She could no longer be a light unto the nations. She could no longer reveal God's declarations to them. She became guilty by not living up to her calling.

Israel was not dedicated to God, her spouse, for the immense task for which He had chosen her. She did not pledge her life to it, but rather perished through self-centered acts of disobedience. She made covenants with other peoples, who seduced her into their sinful ways. Thus, she forfeited the ability to be a source of strength for the nations.

In spite of this disappointment God remained loyal to the covenant, which He had made. Again and again He sent prophets to call His people to return to Him. They painted Israel a picture of her current situation, reminded her of the covenant which she had once made with the Lord, reminded her of what her task was to be. They begged and entreated Israel not to grieve God. Israel did return to God from time to time, but the return was never permanent. Usually she paid no attention to the voices of the prophets.

Since God's chosen people could no longer be reached through pleas and reproaches, He had to use other means to train them for their immense commission. Now He resorted to the means He had threatened to use, when He entered into this covenant. He had said that in case Israel should thwart His plan to be the commissioned people for all peoples by breaking the covenant, He would lead His people along the path of chastisement, of dispersion among all peoples. However, this punishment was only for the purpose of educating them for this commission.[21] If Israel has dwelt among other peoples as an outcast, it was only to bring her to the realization that according to eternal election she could not belong to other peoples. Insofar as she disregarded her election and did not desire to be light and salt for the nations, she was hated and persecuted by other peoples, until she could return to her proper position ordained by God and reestablish the covenant.

God, who "declares to man what is his thought,"[22] has always told Israel beforehand what He was planning to do. When He established the covenant with her, He told her how He would punish her, if she didn't remain loyal to the covenant. Therefore, when she was miserable and hated by other peoples, she knew that it was the Lord's doings. The Lord said "Behold the former things have come to pass."[23] Therefore, such events, which befall His chosen people, are not misfortunes and calamities, but are rather the reply of God, their Lord, to their behavior. Yes, God commissioned His messenger, the prophet Ezekiel, to say to His people: "And the nations shall know that the house of Israel went into captivity for their iniquity, because they dealt so treacherously with me that I hid my face from them and gave them into the hand of their adversaries, and they all fell by the sword."[24]

Still the love of God continues to wrestle on behalf of His people. Even in the hour of His deepest disappointment in Israel He makes an oath to His people: "Thus says the Lord, who gives the sun for light by day and the fixed order of the moon and the stars for light by night ...: If this fixed order departs from before me, says the Lord, then shall the descendants of Israel cease from being a nation before me forever."[25]

God is not inconsistent; He does not change His plans and resolutions. Israel's actions cannot embitter His love towards her. And so He continues to strike her with blows of love to rear and educate her for the great commission, which He has entrusted to her. He leads her along the path of correction, as He promised He would, if she should not remain loyal to her commission, to the covenant and the Ten Commandments.

God led Israel out of her land into Assyria and Babylon. When she ignored the voices of the prophets and of Jesus, she was dispersed among all peoples. This method of chastisement, the dispersion among the peoples, was not meant for the destruction of Israel, but for the preparation of His people for the great commission, which could not be accomplished in any other manner. For the Lord has said: "I will make a full end of all the nations among whom I scattered you" — and He has already done this to many peoples who have perished during the course of history — "but of you I will not make a full end."[26]

And indeed He did not make a full end of Israel — as He prophesied. It is a miracle that Israel still exists, that she did not perish among the other peoples. They hated, despised and reviled the people of God. Hitler swore that He would destroy them. Yet, God had decreed otherwise. God protected His people in order to preserve them for their immense commission, to be a light and a bearer of the message for all peoples. Two thousand years — a period of dispersion among all nations, a period of persecution, of massacre and endless heartache — when would Israel's mission become visible?

And now in our days something inspiring is happening. The great turning-point, the end of the period of chastisement has been reached. Israel has returned home to the land of her fathers — a great, meaningful hour. The time has come for her to take up her commission for all the world.

WHY SUFFERING?

Why has the hour of the turning-point come now, in our times? How are we to understand that God is now on Israel's side and fights on behalf of Israel? God had not fought on Israel's behalf for two thousand years, but rather permitted her to endure sufferings and horrible persecutions among the peoples, sufferings and persecutions the likes of which have seldom been seen. Why is Israel now experiencing that God, Who has hidden His countenance from His chosen peoples for two thousand years, looks upon them today with grace and favor? Does this hour, like the hour in which God established the covenant with Israel, have a special significance?

The course of history will take its turn towards judgment in our time, because "the vats overflow, for their wickedness is great,"[27] because evil has reached its peak. However, Israel will experience just the opposite. If the vats of wickedness among the nations are now beginning to overflow, the vats of suffering for Israel, yes, two thousand years of suffering have recently reached their worst in the most dreadful concentration camps, are beginning to overflow. Now the hour has arrived, where the people of Israel have suffered enough in exile for their sins. "Measure by measure, by exile thou didst contend with them; he removed them with his fierce blast in the day of the east wind. Therefore by this the guilt of Jacob will be expiated."[28] Thus says the prophet Isaiah.

Guilt and sin — even when they are forgiven — still carry a punishment with them. When they are forgiven, the punishment is milder through grace. But where there is no repentance of guilt and sin, God often has to lead people through prolonged sufferings to bring them to the recognition of their guilt. A good example of this is Jacob — Israel. He had to atone for the guilt of his craftiness and deceit, by which he cheated his brother out of his birthright. He had to serve Laban for fourteen years for the right to marry his daughter Rachel. Because Joseph was vain and conceited, he had to become a slave and a prisoner before he could be placed into his high post of honor at Pharaoh's court, the post which God had ordained for him from the beginning. And Joseph's brothers had to atone for their grievous sin against him. They had to endure fear and anguish at Pharaoh's court before they could recognize their guilt. These are divine laws, enacted in the history of Israel, as an example to the nations.

However, when the time of chastisement, the time of God's wrath, is over, and the time of purification has been completed, God's anger is transformed into grace, and He says: "Comfort, comfort my people, says your God . . . that she has received from the Lord's hand double for all her sins."[29] Comfort should follow chastisement and suffering, because God's heart is full of sympathy. He sympathizes even when He has to punish and He longs for the hour when He can comfort and cheer. How the Lord must have waited for this hour, when finally the time was fulfilled and His people could return into their land and He could give them their inheritance! How He must have longed for the day, when He could bring them back into the city of Jerusalem where His temple once stood! And all the generations of His people, who only knew suffering and judgment during their lifetime, rejoiced with Him from the other world, as they too watched the events, which ushered in a period of grace for Israel. They will rejoice, when the consolation comes and they will partake of it profusely.

The turn of events in Israel is not due to coincidence nor to fate. It is not due to the fact that God is an inconsistent God, sometimes appearing to be merciful and sometimes angry. But rather, the course of events has taken this turn in accordance with the holy and just laws of God, for Israel and for the world.

At first God grants grace because He wants to let everything come to maturity. He waits patiently until the last possible moment, to see whether the godless will repent, to see whether a people will return to Him. But, then, when the measure of transgressions has reached its peak, He acts justly, according to His decrees — just as Israel experienced it during the dispersion of the last two thousand years after the destruction of the temple. Still, because this holy and just God is at the same time a God of love, it is His plan that a period of grace should begin after His people has suffered the full measure, even though the process of purification must continue until His plan for His people has reached perfection.

IS GOD ON ISRAEL'S SIDE OR NOT: A CRUCIAL QUESTION

The path of Israel proclaims only one thing: The fate of a people depends upon whether God stands for or against them, whether He hides His countenance from them, or whether He looks upon them with grace and favor. If God is for a people — as we saw that He was for Israel during the Six Day War — who can be against them? No one! For no power is greater and stronger than God, the Lord and Master of all, Who has created heaven and earth!

However, God is a righteous God and His relationship to a people — whether He stands for or against them — does not depend upon capriciousness. Rather, His attitude towards them depends upon their relationship to Him and to other people. To be sure, God sometimes gives a people a period of grace, even when their behavior does not warrant it, if they have trodden the path of suffering for the sake of atonement. God is now standing by His chosen people, because they have suffered for thousands of years. However, in the deepest and most ultimate sense He can only give His grace to those who desire it and who need it. And when He now grants a provisional period of grace, this should be recognized as a call to reexamine one's relationship to Him. In spite of provisional periods of grace and periods of grace which let sin mature, God's holy ordinance remains unchanged.

If a people falls away from God — as Israel often did in the course of history and as the Christian peoples are now falling away from Him — He can no longer be for that people, but must declare Himself to be against them. Of Israel it was once said: "But they rebelled and grieved his Holy Spirit; therefore he turned to be their enemy, and himself fought against them."[30] Even though it is very painful for God, He cannot do otherwise than bring His anger and judgment down upon the rebellious people, as He is now threatening to do to the nations.

In God's acts of grace and judgment we come face to face with His righteousness, which no one can escape, not even he who does not believe in God, nor he who denies Him, nor he who rebels against Him. God acts justly. He is righteous. He remains true to His word, which is Yea and Amen. Through a covenant He and His beloved chosen people made an agreement with each other.[31]

God's message to His chosen people is "See, I have set before you this day life and good, death and evil. If you obey the commandments of the Lord your God which I command you this day, by loving the Lord your God, by walking in his ways, and by keeping his commandments and his statutes and his ordinances, then you shall live and multiply, and the Lord your God will bless you in the land which you are entering to take possession of it.

But, if your heart turns away, and you will not hear, but are drawn away to worship other gods and serve them, I declare to you this day, that you shall perish; you shall not live long in the land which you are going over the Jordan to enter and possess. I call heaven and earth to witness against you this day, that I have set before you life and death, blessing and curse; therefore choose life, that you and your descendants may live, loving the Lord your God, obeying his voice and cleaving to him."[32]

God's words to Israel — the promise of blessing and the threat of curse — are unmistakably clear: He will lead her into periods of grace or judgment depending upon her relationship to Him. And He has acted accordingly in the course of history. Israel should be an example to the world, an example of how God's holy ordinances work — in good and evil. The following is an historical example of how God acts according to His ordinance.

Once when Jerusalem was threatened by the approaching Assyrian army and the fate of the city was already sealed, a completely unexpected turn of events occurred. How? King Hezekiah realized that the only way for Israel to win this battle was for her to have God on her side. He commanded the priests and the Levites and all the people to return to God. For he knew that only then could God's fierce wrath be changed to grace and only then would the Lord fight on behalf of Israel.

And so it happened. The priests and the Levites confessed their shame and consecrated themselves to the Lord. The people began to tithe again and to return to God. And even though the outcome of the battle looked hopeless, King Hezekiah was able to address his subjects: "Be strong and of good courage. Do not be afraid . . . for there is one greater with us than with him. With him is an arm of flesh; but with us is the Lord our God, to help us and to fight our battles."[33] Israel experienced a brilliant victory and the Assyrians became a laughing-stock because of their contempt for the God of Israel.

The whole history of Israel is proof that everything depends upon one's having a right relationship to God. This people experienced victory, success and prosperity, when they stood close to God. Their relationship to Him determined whether they experienced grace or judgment.

God has used Israel as an example to show that the growth and success of every people depends upon whether God is for them or not. If God stands against a people, because they have become ripe for judgment, He uses evil rulers and nations at first to try to bring them to their senses. The prophets tell us this.[34] If this method does not bring results and if the cup of evil is overflowing, no power, no alliance can help that people. It is true that the military strength of the people seems to be the decisive factor in war, but God makes the final decision as to whether a people will experience victory or defeat — according to His plan, according to what He deems best for the upbringing of that people.

How overwhelming is the love of God! Even in spite of our greatest transgressions He seeks ways and means so that we will not have to forfeit the election which He has granted to us. His hands are shaping the whole history of the world in such a manner, that His beloved Israel, His son, His child, as He calls him, can grow into the dignity of his unique election. His love knows no bounds. It finds no rest, until He can shower all of His grace upon His beloved son.

By observing the path of Israel through time we catch a glimpse of the Being of God, which is Holiness and above all Love. We see that behind all of God's actions — His pardons and corrections — He has a wondrous plan, a plan which we can recognize in retrospect.

THE ONSET OF THE MESSIANIC KINGDOM

What is the plan for Israel now in our time? We have just recognized that we have entered into the last times. But the last times have several different phases. It is necessary to recognize whether a phase is beginning or coming to an end. The great turning-point of Israel's course, which is marked by the foundation of the state of Israel and also by the unification of the city of Jerusalem, signifies the beginning of the last days, whose consummation will be the Messianic Kingdom. The period of grace for Israel has begun, but it has various stages. For example, first Israel became a state and received her land. Then she received the old city of Jerusalem. The Messianic Kingdom will be the coronation of the period of grace, which began in Israel in 1948.

That does not mean, however, that the Messianic Kingdom has begun to appear. The head rabbi of the Israeli army, Shlomo Goren, saw the situation differently as he stormed the wailing wall, erected the torah scroll there and blew the Shofa-horn. He announced to the world, that the city of David was now again in the hands of the Jews and solemnly declared: "We are entering into the Messianic Age." However, he is right only insofar as this period of grace will lead to the Messianic Kingdom, but the sequence of events has only just begun.

The "bones" of Israel, as the prophet Ezekiel prophesied for the last days, have returned into their land! "Therefore, prophesy, and say to them, Thus says the Lord God: Behold, I will open your graves, and raise you from your graves, O my people; and I will bring you home into the land of Israel."[35] This has begun to happen; the outbreak of God's grace over Israel has begun. But in the bones there is no breath — the quickening spirit of God is not yet in them. And the prophet Ezekiel says quite clearly that the coming together of the bones belongs to the first phase. This regathering is the gift of grace to God's people.

But after this prophecy has been fulfilled, a second event occurs and this typifies the entrance into the Messianic Kingdom. The Lord commands: "Come from the four winds, O breath, and breathe upon these slain, that they may live." "And I will put my spirit within you, and you shall live."[36] The event which triggers the outbreak of the Messianic period among His people is therefore an outpouring of the Spirit. The fact that Israel could sense the wonderful help of God after her victory does not signify a spiritual revival. The sign of a spiritual revival is a deep and painful remorse because they did not really believe in God before, because they didn't give Him the honor, because they didn't love Him above all, because they didn't consecrate their lives to Him.

The quickening Spirit of God shows us where we have not placed our will, our strength, our talents, money and goods at His disposal, where we have not lived according to the proclamations of His will, and where we have not hated our sin. Out of this remorse comes our dedication of love to God. A moving example of this occurred during the reign of Josiah, who together with all his subjects wept over his sins during the reading of the Torah. They repented, destroyed their idols and renewed the covenant with the Lord.[37] Only with such a revival can the onset of the Messianic Kingdom begin. The kingdom itself can't begin until the Messiah, the King of this kingdom, has appeared as the Anointed One of God.

This means that the Messianic Kingdom will

not begin with a military victory, with the possession of the land of the fathers or of the whole city of Jerusalem. The Messianic Kingdom is the "Kingdom of God" — a kingdom of peace, of joy, of righteousness, of prosperity. Such a kingdom can only begin when the citizens have become a new people. If there is a disposition of indifference, pride, envy, hate, or depravity, or if there are other sins which the citizens do not fight against, then the kingdom of peace and prosperity cannot become a reality. A kingdom of peace and prosperity with citizens who do not fight against sin would be utopia. Sin always brings with it misfortune, enmity, strife, war. An inner renewal, which begins with remorse and repentance, is necessary so that the Messianic Kingdom can begin and so that the Messiah can find subjects for His kingdom of peace. Remorse and repentance — as we can see in the history of Israel and in the lives of individuals — occur when God lays His finger on the foul and sinful spot in our human nature and judges us. That is why this period — even if God's sun of grace has already risen and is shedding its beams upon Israel — can only be a period of preparation and purification for the coming Messianic Kingdom.

ISRAEL IN THE DECISIVE EVENTS OF THE LAST DAYS

The last days as a time of preparation for the Messianic Kingdom will bring to Israel several outstanding, decisive events: First, the invasion of the eastern powers; then, the advance of the anti-God world power and the world dominion by the son of perdition, as foretold by the prophet Daniel for the first part of the last week of years; finally, the march of all nations to the Battle of Armageddon and the judgment of the nations. All of these events will be the prelude to the Messianic Kingdom.

THE INVASION OF THE
EASTERN POWERS

The last days will be filled with wars. Lawlessness and sin, hatred and strife, greed and
the desire for power are on the increase.
Finally man will no longer be afraid to use
every means at his disposal to obtain the
power he desires. The whole world will be
entangled in a war which will develop into a
total conflagration. Stangely enough these
wars will not concern the east-west conflict,
but rather, Jerusalem, which has already become a focal point of international events and
which will remain a focal point right down to
the last days. (That became clear at the declaration of truce at the United Nations on
July 7, 1967.)
Immense and powerful troops from many different nations will descend upon Jerusalem in
our time, in the beginning of the last days.
As the Bible prophesies, they will come pri-
marily from the north and the east.
The invasion of these hostile troops into the
land of Israel is described in the book of the
prophet Ezekiel.[1] The passage is concerned

with Gog, the prince of Mesech and Tubal, whose domicile lies far away in the north. His army will come like a storm, like a cloud covering the land.[2] It is a type of Blitzkrieg. Israel will be taken unawares. The invading armies will be permitted to proceed up to the mountains of Israel, and then the Lord will intervene.

According to the prophetic words, the assault of the enemy will take place in our time, in the time when Israel has returned home to her land, in the time which is generally described as "the last time." This is the prophetic vision: "After many days you (Gog) will be mustered; in the latter years you will go against the land that is restored from war, the land where people were gathered from many nations upon the mountains of Israel, which had been a continual waste: its people were brought out from the nations ... you will come up against my people Israel, like a cloud covering the land. In the latter days I will bring you against my land ... O Gog ..."[3]

No power on earth will be in the position to stand against these mighty armies with all of their allies, let alone the small nation of Israel. She is, of course, given up for lost and surrendered to destruction. We are standing in the last times, the times which brought about the great turning-point for Israel, the beginning of God's grace over His people. "On that day there shall be a great shaking in the land of Israel . . . and the mountains shall be thrown down, and the cliffs shall fall, and every wall shall tumble to the ground. I will summon every kind of terror against Gog, says the Lord God; every man's sword will be against his brother. With pestilence and bloodshed I will enter into judgment with him; and I will rain upon him and his hordes and the many peoples that are with him torrential rains and hailstones, fire and brimstone. So I will show my greatness and my holiness and make myself known in the eyes of many nations. Then they will know that I am the Lord."[4]

There will be a complete defeat of the enemy on the mountains of Israel, because the Lord calls the mountains of Israel "My mountains" and He will defend His possession. Yes, He calls Israel "My people," again. He has reaccepted them, after leading them along the path of chastisement, in order to prepare them for the great commission.

Because God is the God of Israel, He fights with His strong arm against Gog and his allies, so that contrary to human understanding the enemy is defeated on the mountains of Israel.

That will overwhelm His people even more than the victory of the Six Day War. There will be even more praise and thanksgiving for the miracle. Not only in Israel, but also in all the other nations people must recognize that this is a miraculous deed of God. Yes, the Lord accomplished this, "that the nations may know me, when through you, O Gog, I vindicate my holiness before their eyes."[5] God has magnified His holy name — just as He did, when He destroyed Pharaoh's troops in the Red Sea — so that all the world could see: God has intervened! The enemy, with millions of troops, armed with the latest weapons, with many nations for allies, has attacked a tiny nation, whose country is not as large as the head of a straight pin on the map, and yet the enemy could not defeat her. Then the nations must recognize that the victory has occurred in a miraculous manner, as the Lord has spoken: "And I will set my glory among the nations; and all the nations shall see my judgment which I have executed."[6]

The last days which are now dawning over Israel are the time of her preparation for the Messianic Kingdom. It is a time in which God lays great importance upon remorse, repentance and return to Him. The period of time during which God turned His countenance away from Israel is over. He is now gracious to her. He saves her from her enemies just as He will save her from this fierce enemy with all of his allies. However, for the sake of purification Israel must undergo further trials of fears and anguish.

These fears and afflictions will cause many people in Israel to turn to the Lord, to cry unto Him, to seek His face. They will promise to turn over a new leaf, to forsake their old ways, ways which separated them from God and which ended in the transgression against the declarations of His will. When His grace is revealed, everyone will recognize that the Lord of Israel is God, that Israel's exile among the peoples was no accident, no blind twist of fate, but rather an act decreed by God in reply to the behavior of His people. Through this people will recognize how holy God is, and how stringent His demands on Israel are, the people whom His love has chosen for the highest commission. They are very precious and dear in His sight.

During the time of the enemy invasion of Israel, during affliction, distress and fear, there will be a preliminary separation, like the separation which will occur on the day of the Lord, when the Messiah comes and establishes His kingdom. The Lord will take into the Messianic Kingdom only those members of the house of Israel, who are of a broken and contrite heart, who like David have continually repented, loved their Lord, and prepared themselves for His coming.

In the days of terror, when Gog and his allies descend like a cloud upon the country of Israel, only those who are standing in a right relationship to God will experience aid and rescue. Either they will experience external protection through miracles and divine interventions, or, if the Lord calls some of the God-fearing in the land of Israel to Himself, He will let them be borne home in peace on the wings of angels. The God-fearing will experience the protection of the God of Jacob, Who comforts us in His lap, as a father comforts his children, during a storm.

Now that this ominous war is standing before us, it is of the utmost importance, whether we are God-fearing, whether the relationship of the people Israel and of each and every Israeli is one of love toward his God. For we have seen in the course of history that God's decision as to whether He would show favor or not depended upon the behavior of the people, whether they kept the covenant of love, obeyed His ways and led their lives in accordance with His commandments.

When the onslaught of the enemy with terrible, perhaps with atomic, weapons occurs, it will then be too late to change one's relationship to God. It will be too late to dedicate one's life to God. There will be no more time left to profess Him as Lord, to practice the First Commandment, to love Him above everything else, and to faithfully live out the other commandments. What one experiences when the destruction and the onslaught of the enemy take place will depend upon one's personal relationship to God. Either he will be hidden in God, like in a fortress, and comforted, so that there will be peace in his heart or he will be blown about like a leaf in a storm, at the mercy of the horrors of war.

Today, the decision is made as to what will await me in the coming war: whether or not I will experience such peace, as many experienced during the horrors of the last World War. A British pilot, Charles Coward, who was shot down in Germany and was taken into the concentration camp at Auschwitz and who rescued many Jewish children there, reported many such cases. He saw Jewish women going to death singing and praying with divine radiance and peace on their faces. Full of joy, like people going to a wedding, they entered into the gas chambers.

God has promised this heavenly peace to those who love Him and who do His will — "O that you had hearkened to my commandments! Then your peace would have been like a river."[7] — it is as though God lifts them completely out of the horror which drives others to despair.

No one knows how long or how short the time will be between the Six Day War and the next war, which may be the decisive one prophesied by Ezekiel. Yet, we must assume that the time span is short. No one can afford to rest on the laurels of the last victory, to forget to thank God for His miraculous intervention by dedicating his life to Him. Perhaps some of the Israeli soldiers broke out crying when they saw the wailing wall and prayed to God as they had never before prayed in their lives. Perhaps they made a vow to Him because of His divine aid during the war. Whoever, soldier or civilian, made a vow at that time and is not keeping it now, but has returned to his old ways, ways of indifference or sin, has forfeited his chance for reprieve in the next war. The overwhelming grace of God, which granted Israel victory during the Six Day War, is a call to each member of His people to surrender his life to the Lord. Whoever misses this chance is missing something very important and is losing that which would make him strong for the difficult times which lie ahead.

God didn't grant the powerful victory of Israel, so that they could take a spiritual vacation, separate themselves from God and become languid in thanksgiving and devotion. Furthermore, God did not give Israel victory, so that she could be pleased with her own efforts and proficiency and nourish her pride. Then God would have to humiliate her again. No, God granted the grace of victory, so that His goodness could lead them to a renewal of heart. God has in mind the Messianic time, which is quickly approaching. He wants to prepare this generation. It must live resolutely towards this end, which is drawing ever closer. The Messiah is coming.

And so God continues to act in order to prepare and purify His people. Through His magnificent victory over the powerful enemies which Ezekiel prophesied, His glory and majesty will be manifested. Many people, especially in Israel, will be brought to their knees to confess their sin and to dedicate their lives to the Lord. However, the number will be few and the repentance and dedication will not be deep enough. Yet God will not forsake His people. He will continue to seek them until He reaches His goal.

Wonderful plans of God lie behind the school of preparation, behind wars and afflictions, plans which contain destinies of glory for His people. For, when the Messianic Kingdom begins, Israel will emerge as the bearer of blessing for God, She will pass on great commissions and blessings for mankind. She will become the missionary people for all peoples.

THE SON OF PERDITION
REACHES MATURITY

As deepest night must precede the splendor of dawn, so the world must pass through the darkest part of the night before the glory of God is manifested. The cup of affliction must overflow, before solution and salvation appear. An example of this is Israel's narrow escape from Pharaoh through the Red Sea. Up until the last minute, it looked as though they would perish at the hands of the Egyptians. God is letting every situation reach its peak in order to show men that it is He alone Who can grant aid, solution, and the true kingdom of peace. Before the Messiah appears and before the Messianic Kingdom begins, the son of perdition, the man of sin, will appear. According to the prophet Daniel's declaration, he will proceed out of the fourth and most frightful "beast," which comes out of the abyss. Daniel calls him the "horn."[8] The powers of darkness are appearing in human form and are bringing a visible hell to earth. Satan is embodied as the "lawless one," — who "shall think to change the times and

the law," as the rebel and hater of all that
is divine: God Himself and all who belong
to Him. "He shall speak words against the
Most High,"[9] and his hate will be especially
directed against God's chosen people.

The seven years, the weeks of his power, of
which the prophet Daniel speaks,[10] consist of
two phases. Each consists of three and a half
years. These units of time do not necessarily
correspond to our calendar years, but rather
they are units of time between critical points.
In the first phase he develops his strong position under a mask. In the second phase he
reveals his true nature and begins to work in
earnest. The prophecies of Daniel, which upon
first glance seem to apply to the appearance
of Antiochus Epiphanes (176—164 B. C.), are
multi-stratified and quite definitely apply to
the coming son of perdition, even if the prophecy is not applicable in all respects. That
the statements about Antiochus Epiphanes
also apply to the son of perdition for the last
days, we can recognize by the fact that the
phrase "at the end of time" appears over and
over again. The angel, who gives him the
revelation, says: "Understand, O son of man,
that the vision is for the time of the end."[11]
Not until after the prelude will the son of
perdition publicly take command of mankind.

His power and influence will increase and his pride will develop, until he gains a monopoly of power over all peoples and ascends to his throne. That is the beginning of the anti-God world dominion, which will have great significance for the last days and for Israel.

VOICES OF THE LAST PROPHETS

However, before the son of perdition comes to his real take-over of power, many wars and skirmishes and decisive events for Israel and Jerusalem will take place. God is thinking especially of His beloved chosen people in this hour of the last days, in the battle between heaven and hell. He sends them messengers, who are more powerful than the powers of darkness. We are all acquainted with the prophetic declaration that Elijah will come, before the great and terrible day of the Lord comes. He is the powerful preacher of repentance. He has the task to bring about conversions, to turn the hearts of the fathers to their children and the hearts of the children to their fathers.[12] This special task in the face of the last hour does not surprise us. For even today, at the beginning of the last days, one of the main sins is the unnatural estrangement between children and parents, an estrangement which often turns to hate. It is a rather universal phenomenon.

John prophesied something similar for the last

days, namely that shortly before the anti-God ruler takes over Jerusalem, "two witnesses" will appear in sackcloth.[13] That is, they will be preachers of repentance, who will be equipped with great authority from God to perform miracles and signs. The usual interpretation is that the two witnesses are Moses and Elijah. God does not send these two prophets into the metropolitan cities of the world, but into His beloved city of Jerusalem. His chosen people are to hear the call of the coming of the Messiah, of the true Messianic Kingdom. They are also to hear the call of the day of God's revenge, which will, of course, strike those in Israel who do not heed the call to repentance in the last hour.

In the first three and a half years of the anti-God week Jerusalem will experience great and wondrous things, which will turn the world upside down. The last trumpet blast will be heard in Jerusalem, before the son of perdition takes over the world dominion. The lives of the two witnesses, their deeds and their messages, will be a testimony to all mankind. Their death will probably be announced worldwide on radio and their corpses viewed on television.

The appearance of the two witnesses shows something of the great love of God towards

His chosen people, insofar as the deeds of the witnesses will give everyone in Israel another great opportunity to equip himself for the coming times. After the last trumpet call of the Anointed One of God, the anti-God ruler will seize power in the second phase of the anti-God week of years. This time will be unspeakably difficult for Israel. It will bring with it the most difficult hardships because the man of godlessness hates God's people, and he wants to destroy them. Now that he has gained control over the world dominion, he seeks ways to proceed against Israel.[14]

THE PSEUDO-MESSIAH
IN THE TEMPLE

The world dictator is a great liar, like Hitler, his predecessor. Therefore, he will most likely not lay his cards on the table at the beginning of the game, but will hypocritically pretend to be pious. In his deceitful arrogance, mimicking the divine, he will assert that he has come to establish a kingdom of peace, resembling a "kingdom of God." Like Hitler, he will make speeches about an "eternal kingdom," about a "kingdom of peace."

Jerusalem has been designated as the center of the Messianic Kingdom, the city of the king of peace. Therefore, the son of perdition will strive to enter the city and hold forth his proclamations as a pseudo-messiah. And so he will probably march through Israel and set up camp there, as would be fitting for the Messiah to do, in order to proclaim his message to mankind from Jerusalem.

By that time, the temple will have been rebuilt according to the prophecy of Hosea, who said that Israel would be without a temple and priests for a long time, until the last days.[15]

Since the whole world knows that the temple is the seat of God, the son of perdition forces his way into the temple to set up his throne there, after a manner of speaking. He wants to have the satisfaction that he, sitting in God's house, has deposed God, that mankind will listen to his message instead of to God's teachings.

And so the dreadful thing will happen, of which Daniel prophesied[16] and of which Jesus spoke in His speech about the last things: "the desolating sacrilege ... standing in the holy place ..."[17] The son of perdition will enter the temple of God and pretend that he is God. One can imagine him sitting on the throne holding his eloquent pleasant-sounding speeches, exciting the world with his seemingly beneficent messages of peace and prosperity — the whole scene broadcast on world-wide television.

Then he will probably introduce a pious cult into the temple to satisfy his desire for recognition. In his deceitful manner, he will probably use divine concepts and even quote from the Word of God. However, when he speaks of God, he usually means the man who is equal to God, ultimately himself. Men need religion. Therefore, those who have fallen away from God will probably turn with great enthusiasm to this new cult inspired by the devil.

In this time of greatest temptations, when the anti-God ruler will use alluring words to "seduce with flattery those who violate the covenant,"[18] only those who have fervently practiced God's commandment "to love Him above everything else" will be able to endure. The overcomers will be the ones, whose hearts have pulsated with love towards God; whose life, thoughts and feelings have centered around Him; who have done everything out of love to Him, in order to make Him happy; who have lived their lives according to His will and according to the instructions laid down in the Ten Commandments.

This devotion will pay off in the time of trial. The God-fearing have honored truth. They have accepted with humble hearts the verdict and judgment of God over every deed, over every sin. Because they are accustomed to living in truth, they are now able to see the truth about the son of perdition. Before their eyes he is unmasked as the man of lawlessness, of arrogance, of lies and of hate, although he only mentions peace and world brotherhood in his speeches.

TIME OF DEEPEST AFFLICTION

After the time of camouflage the real character of the world ruler is publicly revealed, revealed in the way he proceeds against all God-fearing people: the people of Israel and the God-fearing among the Christians. A consuming hate breaks out of him, because these people belong to God and give honor and love to Him Whom he hates. He knows that he has only a little time left on the earth, before he will be judged by God and destroyed. Then the Messiah will come and set up His Messianic Kingdom and His sovereign authority will proceed from Jerusalem throughout the whole world. Therefore, the anti-God ruler persecutes the God-fearing to the point of death.

Now the prophet Daniel's prophecy for the last days will come true: "There shall be a time of trouble, such as never has been since there was a nation till that time."[19] Daniel writes about how "... this horn made war with the saints, and prevailed over them."[20] It is a devilish war in the truest sense of the word, for here Satan is embodied in the person of a human being, as the son of perdition who has brought hell to the earth. Yes, he "shall wear out the saints of the Most High ... and they shall be given into his hand for a time, two times, and half a time."[21] "They shall fall by sword and flame, by captivity and plunder."[22]

He finds support among mankind for his actions against the God-fearing. Since he is able to rebuild the world, devastated by wars, it seems as though God has laid His confirmation upon his actions and has blessed him. That is why he can afford to take measures against the God-fearing.

He will scourge them as disturbers of the peace, who pray down the judgment of God upon the people through the preaching of repentance and who undermine the kingdom of peace, which everyone yearns for after the dreadful wars. He will impress upon the people the fact that the only way in which the kingdom of peace, the atomic age of prosperity, can be guaranteed is through removal of the disturbers of peace. This is the manner in which he will approach mankind, which in our time is already falling further and further away from God every year, living in rebellion against His commandments, in impulsiveness and in hate. Now people have an object, on which they can take out their hate: the loathsome disturbers of the peace, who are a living accusation by the very lives which they lead and who disturb the consciences of the godless. The son of perdition will find men to carry out his instructions.

So the beginning of the world kingdom of "peace" is the beginning of dreadful persecutions, afflictions and martyrdoms, which have never before been seen on earth, for the extermination of all who belong to the people of God.

The hour directly preceding the coming of the Messianic Kingdom will be the darkest hour for all true members of His people, i. e. for all who stand in the faith of the fathers. Did not the sun of grace rise over Israel? Was not the countenance of anger transformed into a countenance of grace for His people? Yes, and it will remain so. For this darkest hour will also be the hour of many miracles, of answers to prayer and preservation. In spite of all the sufferings, God has not turned His face away from Israel.

It is the time directly before the coming Messianic Kingdom, which is already shedding its light: God is drawing close to His chosen ones and is giving them peace in their hearts — heavenly peace, which the world cannot give. He is also granting them heavenly joy, which mankind cannot experience under the jurisdiction of the son of perdition.

God stands by His chosen people in that He lets them remain in their land and "Jerusalem shall still be inhabited in its place"[23] in spite of numerous wars. And, as we shall see shortly, not many years hence He will make an end of all peoples who march against Jerusalem. Yet He will protect and save His chosen people — to be sure, only those who are God-fearing will endure.

That God bestows His favor upon His people will be proven by the fact that He will grant many marvelous preservations. It is written that 144,000 of the tribes of Israel will be preserved because they are like Noah.[24] Like him they are obedient to God, completely devoted to Him and to His will, no matter what it might cost. It certainly cost Noah a great deal of derision and scorn, as he obeyed God and entered the ark. They are pure souls, who love God with an undivided heart and who do not play the rôle of harlot with the world and men. "God only" is their watchword. Yes, there is no lie found in their mouth. They are blameless and righteous, for they have always honored truth — above all, the truth about their own sinful nature. That is why they can speak the truth about God.

And so they do not nourish the wrath of God, which ultimately is nothing other than the great anguish of God over His sinful children, who refuse to return to Him in spite of all His admonitions and chastisements. However,

God's paths of correction were successful with these certain people, as they were with Noah. What a wonderful prospect! There is salvation in this time of persecution and horror. The ark of Noah will again become a reality, as it was during the first of God's wrathful judgments over the corrupt earth. God will provide a wall of protection, yes, "the Lord is a refuge to his people, a stronghold to the people of Israel."[25] They will experience this refuge in this time of affliction and also later when the wrath of God will rain down upon the other peoples. As the angels once called to Lot: "Hurry, save your soul!," so they are calling to us today, that we may reach the refuge in the difficult times.

When God lets Israel experience such patronage and protection during this most difficult period of persecution under the reign of the anti-God ruler, He will also deem a number of His people worthy to become martyrs. They have the privilege of rendering Him love and honor like no one else during this period of consuming hate, and of praising His name before heaven and earth with their blood shed for His sake. This life witness will pave the way for the coming Messianic Kingdom more than all pious orthodoxy and all pious speeches. Glorious resurrection, coronation and triumph await these witnesses, who have sacrificed their lives.

At the same time, the peoples are tumbling straight down into the abyss in the intoxication of pleasure and of a supposed kingdom of peace, prosperity and happiness. They think that they have escaped the judgments of God and the horrors of war. Yet they are approaching the most dreadful judgment that the earth has ever seen and which will soon overtake them in the Battle of Armageddon near Jerusalem.

Incited by the anti-God world ruler, the
authorities of all the peoples of the world set
out for the battle. They have probably already
reported their victory to the press and to the
radio. What reason will they give — they, the
ones who proclaim a kingdom of peace — for
this contradictory warlike action? In order to
defend and insure peace, they must get rid of
the one agitator, Israel. Perhaps there have
arisen authoritative voices in Israel, which
speak out against the desolating sacrilege or
perhaps there is an underground movement
which is fighting against the world ruler.
Therefore, the world ruler, together with all
the other rulers of the world, whose characteristics are godlessness and lawlessness, yes,
rebellion against God, will strike out with fury
against Israel. They want to defeat this people,
which is for them a sign of God in the world.
Ultimately they want to defeat God.

All the peoples of the earth will assemble
against Jerusalem[26] and set out for the valley
Jehoshaphat, the valley between Jerusalem

and the Mount of Olives. Incalculable numbers of troops march through the wide fields between Meggido and Jerusalem. Hosts upon hosts meet in the valley of decision, while the sun and the moon become darkened and the stars lose their brilliance. This is the picture the prophet Joel paints of the Battle of Armageddon.[27]

Who is it ultimately, who has brought together all these peoples for war? Is it not God Himself? He even says so: "For I will gather all the nations against Jerusalem to battle..."[28] "I will gather all the nations and bring them down to the valley of Jehoshaphat."[29] It is the Lord, Who has assembled here in the valley of Jehoshaphat all the nations of the earth, who are uniting in one more attempt to defeat the people of God and God Himself.

But the Lord laughs at the world ruler's delirium of anger, for the Lord Himself has inspired him to call all the peoples together: "Prepare war, stir up the mighty men . . . Hasten and come, all you nations round about, gather yourselves there."[30] Yes, "they do not know the thoughts of the Lord, they do not understand his plan, that he has gathered them as sheaves to the threshing floor."[31] God has brought together all the peoples, so that, as it is written in the book of Joel, He can reckon with them in the valley of Jehoshaphat, for the sake of His chosen people, His heir, which they led among the nations and divided her land among themselves.[32]

Now the time has come for God to settle accounts with the nations for all that they have done to His chosen people Israel. This is the revenge, which He has been threatening to carry out for a long time. "For the day of vengeance was in my heart ... I trod down the peoples in my anger ... and I poured out their lifeblood on the earth."[33] "I will contend with those who contend with you, and I will save your children. I will make your oppressors eat their own flesh."[34]

Now the hour has arrived when the Lord will sit in judgment over the nations for all that they have done to His chosen people during the last two thousand years. Now the call resounds: "Put in the sickle, for the harvest is ripe."[35] Now is the day of judgment for all peoples. "For as you have drunk upon my holy mountain, all the nations round about shall drink; they shall drink, and stagger, and shall be as though they had not been."[36] Not in vain did the Lord say: "Lo, I am about to make Jerusalem a cup of reeling to all the peoples round about ... On that day I will make Jerusalem a heavy stone for all the peoples; all who lift it shall grievously hurt themselves."[37] "And on that day I will seek to destroy all the nations that come against Jerusalem."[38]

Now Jerusalem will prove itself to be the seat of the throne of God, the city of the Lord of all peoples, as never before. And so, when the peoples march toward Jerusalem, the prophecy of Joel will be fulfilled: "the Lord roars from Zion, and utters his voice from Jerusalem,"[39] to bring judgment upon them. At first Jerusalem will experience great difficulties under enemy attack and she will be partially conquered.[40] This will be His answer to the sin of all those members of His chosen people, Israel, who let themselves be led astray by the son of perdition. However, even during this time, God will stand by His people and let them witness signs and miracles. "On that day the Lord will put a shield about the inhabitants of Jerusalem."[41] "Jerusalem shall still be inhabited in its place, in Jerusalem."[42] And "in Mount Zion there shall be those that escape."[43]

The world ruler, with millions of troops presumably equipped with the latest atomic weapons so that his victory and the extermination of Israel seem inevitable, will not go forth to his day of triumph but to the day of the Lord, as it is written in the book of Joel.

There in the city where the son of perdition had the arrogance to enter the temple of God and to pretend that he was God, the judgment of God will strike him. For the words of the Psalm apply to this army ascending to Jerusalem: "Why do the nations conspire, and the peoples plot in vain? The kings of the earth set themselves, and the rulers take counsel together, against the Lord and his anointed, saying, 'Let us burst their bonds asunder, and cast their cords from us.'" And now comes the answer to these ridiculous undertakings. "He who sits in the heavens laughs; the Lord has them in derision."[44] Only the breath of His mouth, one word, and the whole anti-God army will be destroyed and a dreadful punishment will ensue.

The peoples must now recognize that it is impossible for them to finish off God, to put an end to Him. They must recognize that He is the Lord and Creator of all things, that He has all might and power and that men, His creatures, are like particles of dust in His sight, like drops in a bucket. Now they must recognize that their hour has come; the hour from which no one can escape with his sin; the hour, in which God's judgment will take place. The punishment of the righteous and holy God will strike.

Now His frightened people and all truly God-fearing people on the earth will see that the darkest night at the end of time has brought forth the bright sun. The Messianic Kingdom has arrived. The Messiah has appeared in glory and majesty. Ultimately Satan himself served only to bring about the Messianic Kingdom and to make manifest the victory of God.

THE MESSIAH APPEARS —
THE HOUR OF RECOGNITION

Now the Messianic Kingdom of peace has begun under the rule of Israel — the coming of the Messiah has brought about the turning-point. Now the passage in the Psalms has come true: "I have set my king on Zion, my holy hill. You shall break them with a rod of iron, and dash them in pieces like a potter's vessel."[45] The Messiah has accomplished this. He has brought all the kingdoms of the world under His dominion and from Jerusalem He will rule over them.

The end of history has reverted back to the beginning. The beginning of the history of the world was concerned with Israel, His chosen people. The end of history is also concerned with Israel. The land which Abraham, the ancestor and patriarch of Israel, received as an inheritance for his seed as a holy land, has become the stage upon which the kingdom of the Messiah will be set up. All of the decisive epochs of God's world dominion revolve around this land and the city Jerusalem. That is why the Messiah with His glory and majesty can appear only in Jerusalem to judge the nations and to become King of His people. For only through His appearance can the wonderful plan of God for His people and for the other peoples be carried out.

What will be the characteristics of the Messiah? After the appearance of the pseudo-messiah, of the world ruler, the prince of the alleged kingdom of peace, the character traits of the true Messiah are evident. They are the direct opposites of the characteristics of the pseudo-messiah who has brought ruin and destruction through his arrogance, hate, lies and lawlessness.

The true Messiah bears the trait of divine nobility. He is the Prince of Peace[46] and the truth. He is the Righteous One and the Savior, Whose dignity lies in humility.[47] His rod of iron is meekness. His scepter is mercy. His authority is love. This passage from the book of Isaiah describes the anointed Servant of God: "A bruised reed he will not break, and a dimly burning wick he will not quench; he will faithfully bring forth justice."[48] Because He is light, His task is "to open the eyes that are blind, to bring out the prisoners from the dungeon, from the prison those who sit in darkness."[49] Because He is love, He knows "how to sustain with a word him that is weary."[50] Above all, the Messiah will bear the traits of Jesus. As a Christian I profess to believe that Jesus, Who was born of the Jews, will appear on that day as the Messiah and King of Israel.

How will His people be able to recognize their Messiah? It is written that during the affliction and duress of the battle of Armageddon God's Spirit will be poured out.[51] He is the Spirit, Who will bring remorse and Who will enliven the "bones" of Israel. This is the outpouring of the Spirit which Ezekiel writes about.[52] The prophecy of Zechariah will also be fulfilled: "And I will pour out on the house of David and the inhabitants of Jerusalem a spirit of compassion and supplication, so that, when they look on him whom they have pierced, they shall mourn for him, as one mourns for an only child, and weep bitterly over him, as one weeps over a first-born."[53]

Then Israel will recognize her Messiah — Whom she may imagine differently. His feet will stand upon the Mount of Olives, in whose crevice the afflicted people found shelter.[54] Israel will hail Him, Who has won the victory for her: "Blessed be he who enters in the name of the Lord."[55]

COMMENCEMENT OF THE
MESSIAH'S REIGN

Now the words of David will be fulfilled:
"The Lord says to my lord: 'Sit at my right
hand, till I make your enemies your footstool.'
The Lord sends forth from Zion your mighty
scepter."[56] In this passage it is quite clear that
the Messiah is being spoken of as a person.
It is also clear that He will come from above,
because He is the Anointed One of God. He
will bring a divine, heavenly reign into the
Messianic Kingdom.

That which Daniel once saw in a vision will
become reality: "As I looked, thrones were
placed and one that was ancient of days took
his seat; his raiment was white as snow, and
the hair of his head like pure wool; his throne
was fiery flames, its wheels were burning fire.
A stream of fire issued and came forth from
before him; a thousand thousands served him;
and ten thousand times ten thousand stood
before him; the court sat in judgment, and the
books were opened. I saw in the night visions,
and behold, with the clouds of heaven there
came one like a son of man (i. e. he looked like

a normal man), and he came to the Ancient of Days and was presented before him. And to him was given dominion and glory and kingdom, that all peoples, nations, and languages should serve him; his dominion is an everlasting dominion, which shall not pass away, and his kingdom one that shall not be destroyed."[57] And by this another prophecy is fulfilled: "Judgment was given for the saints of the Most High, and the time came when the saints — i. e. His people — received the kingdom."[58] And so the throne of glory, which the "son of man" occupied in the presence of the Father, will descend upon Jerusalem, for it is written: "At that time Jerusalem shall be called the throne of the Lord."[59]

With the appearance of the Messiah, the Messianic Kingdom has begun. It is a kingdom of peace in contrast to the previous kingdom, which gave only an illusion of peace. The citizens of the previous kingdom lived in sin and indulged in carnal pleasures, in hate, in lies and deceits. The people of God, on the other hand, has been prepared for the Messianic Kingdom. They were prepared through the unspeakable sufferings under the rule of the pseudo-messiah and through the outpouring of the Spirit, which brought them remorse and transformed their hearts. Because the people of Israel now have humble and contrite hearts and because peace and love fill their land, Israel can now become the center of the kingdom of peace and righteousness.

Israel is now really the "people of God." She bears His traits. What God said when He established the covenant with Israel has now become true: "You shall be holy; for I the Lord your God am holy."[60] Now she is living according to His commandments, according to the statutes of the Messianic Kingdom of peace. The center is now the Messiah-King, to Whom His true subjects bring honor and love, and Who, like a good shepherd, leads them into the best pastures. Israel has become the people of blessing for all peoples. Now every prophecy about the Messianic Kingdom of peace has been fulfilled.

ISRAEL'S COMMISSION
OF BLESSING
IN THE MESSIANIC KINGDOM

THE KINGDOM OF PEACE
BELONGS TO THE REDEEMED

The Messianic Kingdom has arrived. There is a burst of joy in the hearts of the redeemed. They can scarcely believe it. They walk about as if in a dream. Only a few hours ago they were living under a satanic ruler, the son of perdition. The atmosphere of evil which encircled them was so thick that the people of God could scarcely breathe. They themselves suffered under dreadful persecutions. The others lived in a world of sin, according to their evil passions and depravities, which brought only devastation and horror.

But now great things have happened. "I will remove the guilt of this land in a single day."[1] The coming of the Messiah brought that about. "On that day there shall be a fountain opened for the house of David and the inhabitants of Jerusalem to cleanse them from sin and uncleanness."[2] "And no inhabitant will say, 'I am sick'; the people who dwell there (in the Messianic Kingdom) will be forgiven their iniquity."[3]

The power of sin has been broken. Redemption has come. Redemption is the word which is written in large letters over the Messianic Kingdom. Israel is a redeemed people. Israel has been reconciled to God. That is why men are living in reconciliation with each other. This reconciliation radiates into the world. It causes other peoples to "beat their swords into plowshares, and their spears into pruning hooks; nation shall not lift up sword against nation, neither shall they learn war any more."[4] That was the picture prophesied for the Messianic Kingdom thousands of years ago — a picture which became more and more inconceivable as time went on, because the peoples lacerated each other more and more in hate and envy and dreadful wars. At the end the world was just one huge battlefield. However, in the Messianic Kingdom the unimaginable has become reality: there is peace on earth. Every weapon has disappeared, has been melted down. This prophecy of peace for the Messianic Kingdom will be fulfilled just as surely as the prophecy for the time preceding the Messianic Kingdom: that peace would be taken from the earth.

Peace now reigns upon the earth, because men have peace with God and forgiveness of sins. There is peace in their hearts, because they are redeemed from their sins and have experienced forgiveness, because they live in reconciliation and love with each other. Therefore, there is no more room for injustice, quarrels, envy or strife due to arrogance or coveting another's possessions or honor. There is no more room for those things which had previously disrupted peace and prosperity. Throughout thousands of years, peace conferences and attempts to make countries tolerate each other have failed. The healing has to come from within. God's peace must rule in the hearts of men through redemption, before there can be peace on earth.

Now the kingdom of peace has arrived, the time for which Jeremiah prophesied: "Behold the days are coming, says the Lord, when I will raise up for David a righteous Branch, and he shall reign as king and deal wisely, and shall execute justice and righteousness in the land."[5] Yes, now that this king from David's root has come, justice and righteousness rule on the earth. Where the Prince of peace has appeared and is accepted, there He will set up His kingdom of peace. In Zion the splendor of righteousness will rise so that all peoples can receive the blessing and peace of the Messianic Kingdom.

The King, the Prince of peace, grants peace to His people. Israel enters into her rest. It is true that "violence shall no more be heard in your land, devastation or destruction within your borders."[6] For where sin has come to an end, devastation and destruction also come to an end. There are no thieves, robbers and murderers, nor innumerable enemies. One can live securely. And so it happens. "My people will abide in a peaceful habitation, in secure dwellings, and in quiet resting places."[7] For "I will abolish the bow, the sword, and war from the land,"[8] as promised — yes, even all evil animals will be driven out of the land, so that "they shall dwell securely, and none shall make them afraid."[9]

Even more — not only will some of the evil animals be driven out of the land, but in the Messianic Kingdom a miracle of transformation transpires: the other evil animals live happily and peacefully in woods and meadows. "The wolf shall dwell with the lamb, and the leopard shall lie down with the kid, and the calf and the lion and the fatling together, and a little child shall lead them. The cow and the bear shall feed; their young shall lie down together; and the lion shall eat straw like the ox. The sucking child shall play over the hole of the asp, and the weaned child shall put his hand on the adder's den. They shall not hurt or destroy in all my holy mountain."[10]

Not only the animal kingdom, but also the plant kingdom, indeed, the whole earth will enjoy the blessed freedom of the redemption of the children of God. The field will no longer bring forth prickly thickets. The earth will no longer be afflicted with floods, nor be withered up by heat waves and droughts. No war will lay the land waste; no insect will eat up the leaves, the blossoms and the fruit.

In admiration and awe men stand before the completion of God's plan for His children. The Messianic Kingdom was in God's mind from the very beginning. In His infinite love His only desire was for the time to become ripe when He could grant a paradise on earth to mankind. This was the goal towards which He had been striving. This was the reason for leading His people along the bitter and painful paths of chastisement. Yes, even those who refused to believe it before, because they stood under the shadow of His blows of punishment, must admit that God is love. Every eye will be opened and will see the goodness of God being spilled forth from His cornucopia down onto His earthly paradise. Men will scarcely be able to comprehend the superabundance of goodness. Yes, it is written: "they shall fear and tremble because of all the good and all the prosperity I provide for it."[11]

Now one no longer has to believe, but one can see with one's own eyes, what the Lord said, "I will rejoice in doing them good."[12]

Like a stream which had previously been obstructed, God's love in all its power and fullness now flows forth over His people. Previously He had to restrain His exuberant love, because like a true Father, He had to lead His son Israel along paths of correction and preparation. However, now everyone can sense the tender love in God's word: "My people will abide in a peaceful habitation." "My people" — all of God's love to Israel is contained in this word.

Yes, Israel has been His people through thousands of years. She is His beloved people, of whom God spoke in the anguish of love: "Is Ephraim my dear son? Is he my darling child? For as often as I speak against him, I do remember him still. Therefore my heart yearns for him; I will surely have mercy on him, says the Lord."[13] Yes, even while God was correcting His people, He had to pause again and again to comfort them. He comforted them with the promises of the prophets: Another time is coming: the Messianic Kingdom is coming; real life is coming.

Then the Lord painted numerous pictures of the Messianic Kingdom before the eyes of His people, so that they could experience a glimmer of joy in their hearts even in the darkest hours. It was their great hope. They lived for the time, in which this kingdom would begin. So the Lord cannot assert often enough: He comes, in order to repay with "oil of gladness instead of mourning," with "a garland instead of ashes."[14] That means that all wars and persecutions, diseases and other forms of suffering will come to an end. It also means that the time of the Messianic Kingdom, the time of joy, the time in which God will requite His people with good things in abundance, has begun. "Instead of your shame you shall have a double portion, instead of dishonor you shall rejoice in your lot; therefore in your land you shall possess a double portion; yours shall be everlasting joy."[15]

Now that Israel has turned herself over completely to God, He no longer has to restrain Himself and hold back His tokens of love. There will be no end to the requital. He will repay Israel for all the humiliation and injustice, which she had to suffer. Truly, "the sons of those who oppressed you shall come bending low to you; and all who despised you shall bow down at your feet; they shall call you the City of the Lord, the Zion of the Holy One of Israel."[16]

Now the nations which had once ridiculed Israel and used the name "Jew" as a term of abuse will bring her honor and praise. "Yea,

I will make you renowned and praised among all the peoples of the earth."[17] "Kings shall be your foster fathers, and their queens your nursing mothers. With their faces to the ground they shall bow down to you, and lick the dust of your feet."[18] What a requital! The highest authorities of the nations will fall down at the feet of Israel! Now they will bow down at the feet of God's people, the holy people, which God has ordained to be His royal priesthood.

GOD'S PEOPLE — CHIEF
OF ALL PEOPLES

Now the sons of Israel will become princes in all the world.[19] Israel will have supremacy over all peoples and will bind them together into a unified kingdom so that the prophecy may be fulfilled: "If you obey the voice of the Lord your God ... the Lord your God will set you high above all the nations of the earth."[20] This was the position that God had ordained for Israel. In order to be worthy of such nobility and to fulfill such a great commission, she must be completely devoted to God. In no other way can she carry out this commission.

Now the hour has come after long periods of chastisement and preparation, after affliction and suffering. So it will come to pass that "you will spread abroad to the right and to the left, and your descendants will possess the nations."[21] "Aliens shall stand and feed your flocks, foreigners shall be your plowmen and vinedressers ... you shall eat the wealth of the nations, and in their riches you shall glory."[22] Now the nations will comply with the demand:

"Sing aloud with gladness for Jacob, and raise shouts for the chief of the nations."[23] Israel is now the chief of all nations. She is their joy, their crown and their ornament. However, the requital goes a step further. All the peoples must recognize Israel as a people blessed by the Lord.[24] The peoples, who have despised and reviled Israel for thousands of years, are now compelled to recognize her righteousness.[25] All the kings will see her glory and honor. They will ascribe to her a new name, a name of honor, which the mouth of the Lord will determine. Now Jerusalem will receive its fame and become a place of praise on the earth for all peoples.[26] Her inhabitants, God's people, "shall be called the priests of the Lord, men shall speak of you as the ministers of our God."[27]

Here in the Messianic Kingdom God's people will fulfill the election which He granted them on Mount Sinai. "You shall be to me a kingdom of priests and a holy nation,"[28] for His people have now received forgiveness for their sins. They are no longer living for themselves or for their idols, but rather they are living for the Lord and for Him alone. They serve Him with love and thanksgiving. "Your people shall all be righteous."[29] All the peoples of the earth will call the "daughter of Zion" the "holy people." Through the coming of the Messiah she has now become what God had ordained for her to become: the redeemed of the Lord.[30]

CITY OF GOD — CENTER OF JOY

Jerusalem shared the fate of the land Israel. As Israel was struck by God and her people were sent into exile, Jerusalem lay barren and waste. Now Jerusalem has the privilege of sharing the good fortune of her people. She will be the center of the Messianic Kingdom. The peoples will make pilgrimages to Jerusalem, to bring praise and honor to God. She will no longer be a deserted city, but rather a city with many visitors, the city of the Messiah-King and the center of the whole world. Songs and shouts of joy will resound in the streets of Jerusalem. No longer is it necessary to arouse the city: "Rejoice, O Jerusalem, behold, your King is coming to you!" Now He has come, He Who brings joy and peace and redeemed life. "Shout, and sing for joy, O inhabitant of Zion, for great in your midst is the Holy One of Israel."[31] "And the ransomed of the Lord shall return, and come to Zion with singing; everlasting joy shall be upon their heads; they shall obtain joy and gladness, and sorrow and sighing shall flee away."[32]

The heart of God, which had to suffer so much with His people on their paths of correction, and with anguish had to ascertain that His people had forsaken Him, now rejoices also. "I will rejoice in Jerusalem, and be glad in my people; no more shall be heard in it the sound of weeping and the cry of distress. For behold, I create Jerusalem a rejoicing, and her people a joy."[33] Here God opens His fatherly heart. He wants to "create Jerusalem a rejoicing" for His people. He wants His people to be joyful, because He rejoices over Jerusalem. He rejoices over Jerusalem, because she has finally attained the position, which He had intended for her. He rejoices, because His people has finally obtained peace.

How God's heart must have ached, whenever His people did not act according to His plans and wishes, whenever they refused to obey His voice! His heart ached, because He had to punish His people. Now the heavens rejoice, for Jerusalem and all her inhabitants are radiant in the splendor of God. The Messianic Kingdom is the kingdom of joy. "I will turn their mourning into joy, I will comfort them, and give them gladness for sorrow. I will feast the soul of the priests with abundance, and my people shall be satisfied with my goodness, says the Lord."[34]

What is the greatest joy? "The earth shall be full of the knowledge of the Lord as the waters cover the sea."[35] "They shall all know me, from the least of them to the greatest, says the Lord."[36] To know God is the greatest joy: to be able to approach the God of love, to live out of His hand, to be guided by His love, to be betrothed and united with Him in eternity.[37]

The great gift was the covenant which God offered to His people on Mount Sinai. "I want to betroth myself with you; I want to be your husband; you shall be my wife. I want to share everything with you. Devote yourself entirely to me." Up until now the Lord has waited in vain for His people to become His wife and to give Him love. But now the great hour has come, the hour of the Messianic Kingdom. With the coming of the Messiah His people are inspired with true love. They turn their hearts over to Him. They establish the covenant anew. Yes, in spite of the fact that the sun will shine seven times brighter in the

Messianic Kingdom and the moon will shine as brightly as the sun,[38] God, the sun of joy, will shine so brightly that the brightness of the sun and the moon will seem pale in comparison. "The Lord will be your everlasting light, and your days of mourning shall be ended."[39] The Messiah has risen over Israel as the light of joy. He has filled the whole land, the heart of every inhabitant with the light and joy and radiance of God. He is the real center of the Messianic Kingdom, the source of all light and joy. Divine radiance proceeds from His people also, because they have become like Him. The heart of God experiences its greatest joy. "As the bridegroom rejoices over the bride, so shall your God rejoice over you."[40] Truly paradise has commenced. It is a paradise of love, which radiates out into all the world and which ushers in a new era: the era of righteousness.

Israel and the rest of the world — what a change in their relationship to each other! Now all the nations love Israel and make pilgrimages to Israel to honor her. The prophecy for the Messianic Kingdom will be fulfilled. "It shall come to pass in the latter days that the mountain of the house of the Lord shall be established as the highest of the mountains ... and many peoples shall come and say: 'Come, let us go up to the mountain of the Lord, to the house of the God of Jacob; that he may teach us his ways and that we may walk in his paths.' For out of Zion shall go forth the law, and the word of the Lord from Jerusalem."[41] Now this passage will become reality. Jerusalem is the center, because all peoples now serve God.

All peoples will now be blessed through and with Israel. The prophecies from thousands of years ago are being fulfilled. "By your descendants shall all the nations of the earth bless themselves."[42] "You are my servant, Israel, in whom I will be glorified."[43] All peoples praise the Lord, because they see His image in the people of Israel. Israel leads the other peoples to the Lord, because she lives only for His sake.

"As you have been a byword of cursing among the nations, O house of Judah and house of Israel (as that indeed was true) so I will save you and you shall be a blessing."[44] And this hour is drawing closer, the hour of the great transformation, of fulfillment. "The inhabitants of one city shall go to another, saying, 'Let us go at once to entreat the favor of the Lord, and to seek the Lord of hosts' ... In those days ten men from the nations of every tongue shall take hold of the robe of a Jew, saying, 'Let us go with you, for we have heard that God is with you.'"[45]

That would not have been possible during the last two thousand years. The peoples would not have come and said: We hear, we see and experience, that God is with you, the Jewish people. No, they would have been more apt to say that God is against His people. Now the tables are turned. All the peoples have seen what has happened: God is with Israel; she is His people. She is a holy people, a people of priests and kings. The peoples come to Israel in order to partake of her blessing. Now the time of the conversion of the nations has come. Throughout thousands of years only individuals have truly become God-fearing. This is also the case in the Christian nations. Only individuals have such a living faith that they let their whole life be determined by God. But now all peoples will be converted to the Lord through Israel. The outpouring of the Spirit at the end of the days, i. e. when the Messiah arrives, is the fulfillment of the prophecy: "I will put my spirit within you, and cause you to walk in my statutes and be careful to observe my ordinances."[46] This Spirit will radiate unto all the peoples, so that they will come and "all the ends of the earth shall see the salvation of our God."[47]

Now, "all the ends of the earth shall remember and turn to the Lord; and all the families of the nations shall worship before him."[48] Now, they will raise their voices and praise the glory of the Lord. "And he will destroy on this mountain the covering that is cast over all peoples, the veil that is spread over all nations."[49] Now, the peoples "shall no more stubbornly follow their own evil heart."[50] And the word of Zephaniah will be fulfilled: "'Yea, at that time I will change the speech of the peoples to a pure speech, that all of them may call on the name of the Lord and serve him with one accord."[51] Yes, "for from the rising of the sun to its setting my name is great among the nations."[52] "Many peoples and strong nations shall come to seek the Lord of hosts in Jerusalem."[53] There, they will hear the ordinances of God and the good news of the redemption and the kingdom of God. There, they will see the glory of God. There, they will recognize the Lord and learn His ways. And the blessing of the Lord will come to all countries.

This picture of the Messianic Kingdom may seem to many in our times to be but a far-fetched dream, a fairy-tale, which has no semblance to reality. However, everything which God has prophesied through His prophets — both threats and promises — has come true. And so His prophecies for the last days and for the Messianic Kingdom will also come true. God's name is "Yea and Amen." He fulfills His promises.

God once said, that if His people did not listen to His voice and did not keep the covenant, He would disperse them among the peoples[54] — and that's exactly what happened. He threatened to have them persecuted and martyred among the peoples[55] — and that also happened. He promised that those who survived the sufferings would return home into the land of their fathers.[56] That happened also in spite of the many attempts to thwart this plan. Yes, in the years before 1948 many people assumed that the plan to exterminate the Jewish people would be carried to completion. Scarcely anyone held it possible that the nation Israel would come into existence. Yet, God fulfills His promises so accurately, that even Jerusalem has now come into the hands of His people.

Now He is about to fulfill the rest of His promises. At first "Gog" with his followers — i. e. a power-block of nations — and then all the nations will march against Jerusalem. Jerusalem will be the center of international events. The prophecies which concern Israel for the time of the anti-God world ruler and son of perdition will also come true. Just as the way is now being paved for the "beast from the abyss," the prophecies for the time after the last days will also come true: the Messiah will appear and the Messianic Kingdom will commence.

The original, wondrous plan of God to give paradise back to mankind will indeed become reality. He will reach the goal which He has set. The Messianic Kingdom will come into being. Sins will be forgiven and the power of the evil one will be broken. Then the Messianic Kingdom will commence and salvation will be brought to the whole world!

God will mold the history of Israel in a marvelous manner, for "He is wonderful in counsel
and excellent in wisdom."

Isaiah 28 : 29

FOOTNOTES

FOOTNOTES

Chapter one (pages 7 to 46)

1   Jeremiah 30 : 11 a
2   Genesis 17 : 8
3   Ezekiel 38 : 8, 39 : 28
4   Zechariah 12 and 14
5   Ezekiel 39 : 7
6   Ezekiel 38 and 39
7   Jeremiah 25 : 32
8   Isaiah 24 : 19 b, 20
9   Isaiah 24 : 20, 5, 6
10 Isaiah 13 : 9
11 Joel 2 : 10
12 Genesis 6 : 11
13 Jeremiah 51 : 7
14 Isaiah 10 : 25
15 Zephaniah 1 : 18 b
16 Isaiah 42 : 6
17 Deuteronomy 10 : 16
18 Genesis 12 : 3 b
19 Isaiah 49 : 6
20 Jeremiah 2 : 19 a
21 Deuteronomy 4 : 25—27; 28 : 15, 25 ff., 64 ff.
22 Amos 4 : 13
23 Isaiah 42 : 9 a
24 Ezekiel 39 : 23
25 Jeremiah 31 : 35, 36
26 Jeremiah 30 : 11

21 Daniel 7 : 25
22 Daniel 11 : 33
23 Zechariah 12 : 6 b
24 Revelation 7 : 1—8; 14 : 1—5
25 Joel 3 : 16
26 Zechariah 12 : 3
27 Joel 3 : 12—16
28 Zechariah 14 : 2
29 Joel 3 : 2
30 Joel 3 : 9, 11
31 Micah 4 : 12
32 Joel 3 : 2
33 Isaiah 63 : 4, 6
34 Isaiah 49 : 25 b, 26 a
35 Joel 3 : 13
36 Obadiah 16
37 Zechariah 12 : 2, 3
38 Zechariah 12 : 9
39 Joel 3 : 16
40 Zechariah 14 : 2
41 Zechariah 12 : 8
42 Zechariah 12 : 6 b
43 Obadiah 17
44 Psalm 2 : 1—4
45 Psalm 2 : 6, 9
46 Isaiah 9 : 6
47 Zechariah 9 : 9
48 Isaiah 42 : 3
49 Isaiah 42 : 7
50 Isaiah 50 : 4
51 Zechariah 12 : 9, 10
52 Ezekiel 37
53 Zechariah 12 : 10
54 Zechariah 14 : 4
55 Psalm 118 : 26

27 Isaiah 61 : 6
28 Exodus 19 : 6
29 Isaiah 60 : 21
30 Isaiah 62 : 12
31 Isaiah 12 : 6
32 Isaiah 35 : 10
33 Isaiah 65 : 19, 18 b
34 Jeremiah 31 : 13 b, 14
35 Isaiah 11 : 9
36 Jeremiah 31 : 34
37 Hosea 2 : 19
38 Isaiah 30 : 26
39 Isaiah 60 : 20
40 Isaiah 62 : 5
41 Isaiah 2 : 2, 3; Micah 4 : 1, 2
42 Genesis 22 : 18
43 Isaiah 49 : 3
44 Zechariah 8 : 13
45 Zechariah 8 : 21, 23
46 Ezekiel 36 : 27
47 Isaiah 52 : 10 b
48 Psalm 22 : 27
49 Isaiah 25 : 7
50 Jeremiah 3 : 17 b
51 Zephaniah 3 : 9
52 Malachi 1 : 11
53 Zechariah 8 : 22
54 Deuteronomy 4 : 25—27
55 Deuteronomy 28 : 64 ff.
56 Ezekiel 11 : 16, 17; 39 : 28

All quotations taken from the Revised Standard Version of the Holy Bible.

Other books by Basilea Schlink
for your further interest

A FORETASTE OF HEAVEN
(American title: I FOUND THE KEY TO THE
HEART OF GOD)
Autobiography, 416 pp. illustrated
We turn the pages as we would the score of
some great symphony and whether the music is
light or whether it is the deep chords that are
struck, our hearts cannot fail to respond. The
response will be an inner searching of our own
hearts and lives followed by love and adoration
for our Lord Jesus. The reader seeking a greater
fulfilment in his Christian life and service will
discover in these pages the key to the very heart
of God.

IN WHOM THE FATHER DELIGHTS   64 pp.
There are times in our lives when God's leadings
seem hard to understand and the heart cries out,
"Why did it have to happen to me? It's almost
breaking me!" Loneliness, perhaps. Disappoint-
ments. A marriage on the rocks. Severe illness
and disablement. Or emotional stress ... Yet
never are we so dear to our heavenly Father as
when we are undergoing trials and chastenings.
As a wise and loving Father He brings us up
carefully, desiring only the very best for us. And
if we trustingly put our hand in His, we shall
find that He has prepared a wonderful outcome
to every path of suffering.

THE UNSEEN WORLD OF ANGELS AND DEMONS   144 pp.

Whether we realize it or not, we are caught up in a colossal battle between light and darkness, good and evil. Neutrality is impossible, for the battle is being fought over us.

Basing her work on the Bible and illustrating her points with many testimonies, Mother Basilea exposes the sinister, destructive purposes of Satan and his demon hordes for mankind. At the same time she depicts the ministry of God's angels. Though we may not usually be aware of their presence, angels are constantly about us, helping, protecting, guiding. They play an active role in human affairs, influencing men and nations, yes, the very course of history.

This book not only shows how they will help us to win the victory in these dark times, but also gives us a glimpse of the love, power, and glory of God as reflected in His holy angels.

MARY, THE MOTHER OF JESUS   128 pp.

Tracing the life of Mary, as we know it from the Bible, Mother Basilea challenges us to a closer walk with Jesus. For have we ever considered that Jesus' first disciple was His own mother? It was Mary who with her Yes to the will of God made it possible for the Saviour of mankind to be born. It was Mary who out of love and humility shared the hardships of His early years and later followed Him to the cross. Many will welcome this heart-warming book, which is written with deep spiritual insight.

RULED BY THE SPIRIT   132 pp.

As in the days of the early Church, described in the Book of Acts, the power of God to guide and inspire individuals who dedicate their lives wholly to Him is still operative today; this is the kernel of Basilea Schlink's challenging message in this book.

THE HIDDEN TREASURE IN SUFFERING
96 pp.

Cares — Strained Relationships — Fear — Illness — Weariness — Loneliness — Inner Conflict — Personality Problems — Unanswered Prayers — Untalented — Growing Old — Want and Need — Fear of Death — Unfair Treatment — Facing Hatred and Slander . . .

From the wealth of her personal experience Mother Basilea Schlink shares how we can find the treasure that lies hidden in every trial and hardship.

FATHER OF COMFORT
(Daily Readings)   128 pp.

These short devotions for every day of the year help us to develop that close contact, a personal relationship of love and childlike trust in the Father, which we need in order to nurture our faith in Him.

"That book has helped me like nothing in this world! I have bought 12 copies and sent them to various friends all over the world. I can't tell you how it has spoken to my rebellious heart, gotten my eyes off people and on to Jesus."

PATMOS – WHEN THE HEAVENS OPENED
128 pp.
In this exposition of the Book of Revelation,
Mother Basilea, as led by the Holy Spirit, focuses
our attention on coming events, which even
now are casting their shadows before them. We
are then shown beyond the sufferings, to the
glory that will follow, to the time when that
great song of eternal praise is centred on the
Lamb that was slain.

REPENTANCE – THE JOY-FILLED LIFE
96 pp.
A remarkable little volume, showing how an
attitude of repentance affects a Christian's inner
and outer life.

THE CHRISTIAN'S VICTORY   192 pp.
(American title: YOU WILL NEVER BE THE
SAME)
How can we overcome sin? Asked this question,
Basilea Schlink set about prescribing "spiritual
medicine", dealing one by one with the sinful
traits which mar the Christian's life, helping us
to recognize them in ourselves, and pointing out
the remedy. We *can* be transformed by gaining
victory over our sins in the power of Jesus
Christ, our risen Lord and Saviour.